DINOSAURS FIGHT TO SURVIVE

Mysterious Death and Discovery in Outback Queensland

ROSE SIVA

All characters appearing in this work are fictitious. Any resemblance to real persons, living or dead, is purely coincidental.

Published by Boolarong Press,
655 Toohey Road
Salisbury Qld 4107
Australia.
www.boolarongpress.com.au

First published 2016

Cataloguing-in-Publication entry available at the National Library of Australia

Creator: Siva, Rose, author.

Title: Dinosaurs fight to survive : mysterious death and discovery in outback Queensland / Rose Siva.

ISBN: 9781925522242 (paperback)

Target Audience: For primary school age.

Subjects: Dinosaurs--Queensland.--Juvenile fiction.

Queensland.--Juvenile fiction.

Printed and bound by Watson Ferguson & Company, Salisbury, Australia

CONTENTS

This story is loosely based on events that really happened, with a fair bit of literary imagination...

Thanks to David Elliot for finding the dinosaur bone at Belmont that started this whole amazing journey, and Lyn and Wendy for their patient persistent proof reading and editing skills.

Thanks to the Australian Age of Dinosaurs for use of their illustrations.

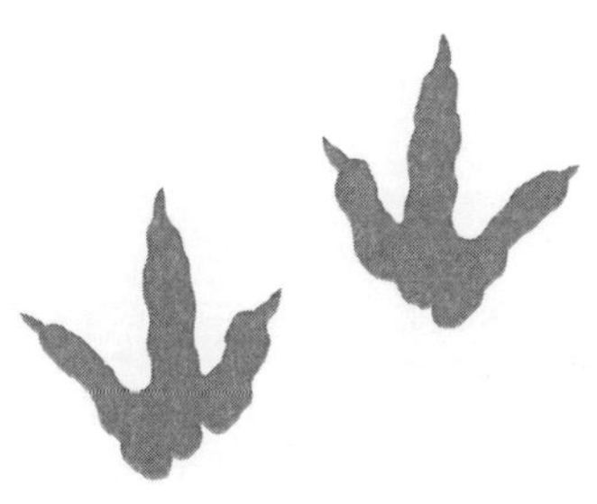

CHAPTER 1

David cursed under his breath as his motorbike slid sideways. Only his quick reactions saved him from falling onto the track. He was on his way out to the back forty acre paddock on Belmont Station in outback Queensland. A third generation farmer, David could 'read' this land like a book, and he thought his farmland looked pretty darn good. After years of drought millimetres of welcome rain had fallen over the past several months. It made the black soil soft and sticky, but it was heaven for the Mitchell grass which had been lying semi-dormant in the dirt. The grass grew centimetres every week, and soon Belmont had been transformed from dry parched paddocks to lush feed lots.

This weather pattern would later be referred to as a 'great dinosaur hunters' season'. When it is dry the black soil contracts and shrinks. When it rains the same soil swells and expands, and this causes the layers in the soil to mix up. Over the years anything caught in the soil is gradually squeezed up to the surface. Even dinosaur bones.

David had sheep on the back forty acres, and he wanted to be sure they were okay and had not got bogged. If they did they could die. He hoped whatever he had hit had not damaged his motorbike. When he got off to check the front wheel he saw a rock, a fair sized rock with a peculiar pattern on it. David had always been observant, a trait extremely important in a farmer. He was curious, so he picked up the rock and put it on the tray of the bike to take back to the farmhouse.

He would look at it later. First he'd check his sheep and then do some repairs on the cattle yards – he was hoping the trucks would be able to get through soon to pick up a load of cattle to take to market. The recent rain had meant Belmont Station had been isolated for several weeks. The postman had been able to get through for the first time yesterday, but he was pretty edgy by the time he got to Belmont. Digging out of and dodging patches of sticky black mud had made his mail run a nightmare. Hopefully, by next week, the road should be dry enough for the trucks to get through.

■■■

After dinner David and his wife Judy examined the rock. It didn't look like other rocks found on the property. It was quite large and unusually heavy, and it had a particular pattern on one edge. David thought he recognised the cellular pattern, he had seen it before on weathered bones of cattle that had died. But this rock was far too big to be a bone from a cow. Far too big, and far too heavy. They turned the rock over, examining all sides. It definitely looked more like a bone than rock. What if?

David and Judy had the same thought at the same time. Was this the remains of an animal bigger than a cow? David had often wondered what this land used to be like thousands or even millions of years ago. He had read that millions of years ago this part of Australia was a great inland sea, and then later covered in vast forests. And it was suggested dinosaurs had lived here. Hard to imagine when you looked at what was here now. What if this bone was a piece of some long extinct inhabitant?

David and Judy were out of their depth. They were farmers – not fossil experts. But the mayor of Winton was interested in fossils, and he knew other people who were experts in that field. David decided he would talk to the mayor of Winton next time he was in town. Little did he know that this find was about to change his life forever...

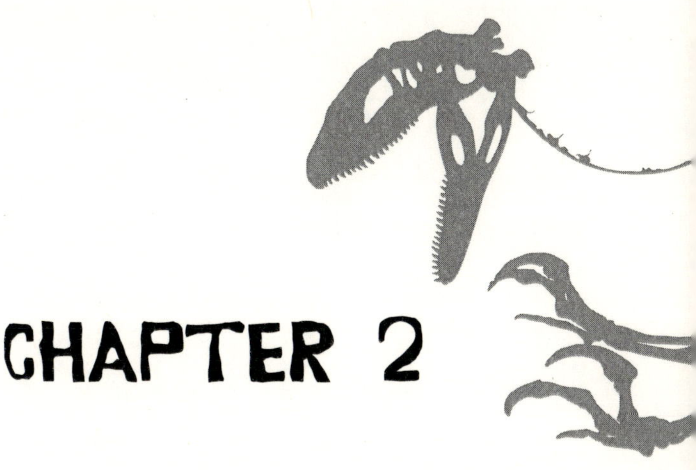

CHAPTER 2

Alex was on his way to Winton on what was probably a wild goose chase. Winton was way out in western Queensland in the Channel Country. It was called the Channel Country because of the numerous streams and rivers that criss-crossed and flooded the country when the rains came. He was familiar with the geology of the Channel Country. One hundred million years ago it had been part of a vast inland sea that formed what is now called the Eromanga Basin. The Great Artesian Basin, a huge underground lake of fresh water, lies under this part of Central Australia. Oil and gas discovered in this part of Australia is evidence that this land was once covered in lush vegetation. It is believed dinosaurs would have lived here back then, and later huge oversized animals called megafauna – the predecessors of the animals we see today.

Alex worked for the Queensland Museum as a palaeontologist. It was his dream job – he had always been interested in geology and as a young child had collected stones and rocks that he kept in shoe boxes under his bed. His mother was always careful to empty his pockets, before she washed his clothes, to save the washing machine from getting damaged. When he was around ten years old someone had given him his first fossil. A rock with a perfectly preserved leaf. It was beautiful – every vein of the leaf was visible, even the delicate serrated edges could be clearly seen. Alex was hooked. This was what he wanted to study when he grew up.

Alex loved doing research and enjoyed studying fossils to determine their age and origin. He also enjoyed going out to remote places on 'digs' to discover more fossils. To him this opened the door to ancient worlds. Australia was unexplored from his point of view – there was so much to learn about Australian ancient history. His job with the Queensland Museum involved a lot of other activities as well – writing scientific papers, arranging new displays, and assessing material people sent in. He was pretty busy.

But now he was heading to Winton, a two day drive west from Brisbane where he worked. Alex was busy with other work, but his boss had pulled rank. Somehow the mayor of Winton had influence at the museum, and Alex was sent to check out a fossil a farmer had found. There had been a few choice fossils found in the area, mostly in caves or washouts, but nothing large. There was evidence of creatures that would have lived in the great inland sea, but not much else. It was believed that, because it was now so dry, any bones in this land would have been reduced to dust eons ago. Bones would have been pulverised, sanded out of existence.

As Alex drove, the land opened up to wide flat plains stretching as far as the horizon. The countryside looked pretty good. Tall grass was growing in the paddocks where healthy looking stock were grazing. Last time he had been out this way the grass was just dry stubble and there was no sign of stock in the paddocks. There had also been a lot of dead kangaroos on the roadside, hit by passing traffic as they grazed what little feed was left. The country had been in drought and the land had been so dry, it was hard to believe anything could live out here. It certainly looked better now.

He turned the radio up to help pass the time. He was still five hours from Winton. This wild goose chase was taking the better part of a week out of his busy life. All because this mayor of a small outback town thought someone had found something interesting. It had better be worthwhile.

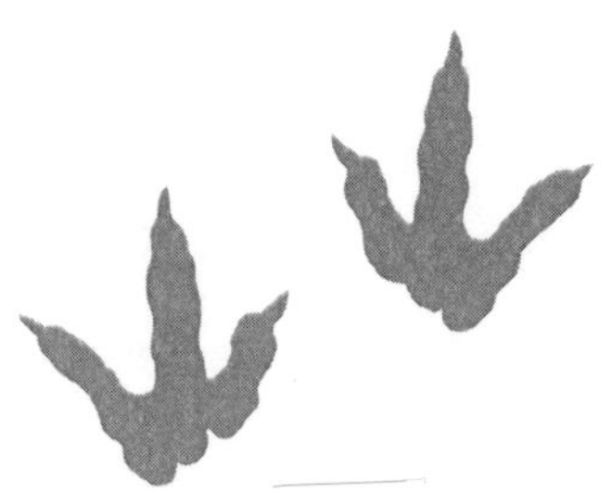

CHAPTER 3

David was waiting. The mayor of Winton had called from his office, introducing Alex to David over the phone. He had also checked the road was open and made sure Alex had the right directions. The drive out to Belmont Station was mostly on a dirt road. Alex didn't mind – he was used to outback roads. The road was still a bit sticky after the rains so he was taking things carefully. He'd had personal experience of getting bogged in Queensland's black soil country and he imagined, with the state of this road, Belmont Station could be isolated for weeks. But so far so good, and it was only a few more kilometres to the station homestead.

When Alex arrived at Belmont, David and his wife Judy welcomed him into the farmhouse kitchen. Judy busied herself making a pot of tea and after some small talk, mostly about the road and the weather, David sat his guest at the large dining table that was the centrepiece of the kitchen.

"I suppose you'd like to have a look at what we found," said David. When Alex nodded David pointed to a lump of something on the far end of the table covered by an old tablecloth. Judy lifted the tablecloth to reveal...

Alex could not believe what he was seeing. Everything he had learned about fossils in outback Queensland said this was not possible. All experts agreed any large fossils would have long been reduced to dust in this hot, arid country. But here was absolute proof this was not so. Absolute proof in the form of the top part of a femur of a massive dinosaur. Alex was speechless. For several minutes they sat in silence as Alex turned the bone over, examining all sides.

■■■

Later that evening David, Judy and Alex sat around the table and talked well into the night. For David and Judy it was a glimpse into a world they had never imagined. Alex described a time when a vast inland sea covered much of this area. This environment would have been perfect for dinosaurs, especially sauropods. As vegetarians they would have needed to eat a huge amount of vegetable matter every day to support their huge bodies.

"How big?" asked Judy.

"Possibly up to thirty metres long, two to three metres tall and probably weighing up to twenty tonnes," replied Alex.

David and Judy's eyes widened in surprise. "What, how could an animal that large survive in land like this?"

"It wasn't like this," explained Alex. "There would have been enormous areas of wetlands and regular rainfall. Massive areas of lush forests would have grown here. We believe some of the largest dinosaurs were herbivores, they only ate vegetable matter."

"Only herbivores?" asked David.

"There were probably carnivores as well, and like all ecosystems the stronger species would have preyed on the weaker species. All would have been part of the food chain beginning with plants."

David struggled to imagine his farmland looking like that. What Alex was describing was so different to what was here now.

In the silence that followed Alex contemplated the future. As far as he was concerned this *had* to be explored further. This was an opportunity to re-write the history books. If it could be proved this was a bone from a huge sauropod it would be a first. It might even be the largest dinosaur ever discovered in Australia. This could prove dinosaurs of this size *had* lived here millions of years ago. But to do that they would have to find more bones.

This would take some serious planning. It would require an organised 'dig' – a careful excavation of the area to see if they could unearth more bones. This bone that had already been found might not be close to any other bones, and they might have to 'dig' over a wide area. The distance from town, and the drive in over a dirt road, might be a problem. If it rained the road could be blocked and they would either not be able to get in or, even worse, not be able to get out. And a 'dig' would require the help of quite a number of people who would have to be involved and looked after. All this would require careful planning.

Gradually a plan came together. David and Judy were prepared to let people stay in their shearers' quarters, and to provide earthmoving machinery to help with a large dig. Alex had access to a group of people he felt could be persuaded to give up their time to travel to outback Queensland to dig in the dirt in the hope of discovering something truly amazing.

Of course he would have to persuade Queensland Museum to allow him to take time out to explore this further. But now he had evidence of what was potentially the largest dinosaur ever discovered in Australia, and it was right here in Queensland.

He felt he had a very persuasive case to present...

CHAPTER 4

Alex's return to the Queensland Museum caused a buzz of excitement. News of a new exciting fossil find quickly spread among the people working in the building.

"Denise," said Alex when he came into the fossil room where she was arranging a new display, "how would you like to be involved in making – or re-making history?"

She looked up, immediately intrigued. "How? Tell me more?"

Denise had always been interested in dinosaurs. Her real life job had nothing to do with dinosaurs or fossils, so she had indulged her fascination by volunteering at the Queensland Museum. Her natural interest and attention to detail made her an ideal 'back room' person, helping to organise and arrange the collections of fossils. She got on well with Alex – he fired up her interest and enthusiasm. He would come back from field trips with all sorts of interesting finds. She had mentioned to him on a number of occasions how much she would like to be involved in the actual discovery of bones in a 'dig'.

"I'm putting together a team of volunteers to go to Winton to see if we can find more dinosaur bones. Would you be interested in being part of the team?"

"Would I ever!"

Alex laughed. "I thought you might be interested. I need people who are able to take a couple of weeks off," he continued. "It will take us a couple of days to drive out there and another couple to drive back, so we would be away for two weeks. Would that be a problem?"

"No, I can organise that. How many are going?"

"I'm hoping to get eight or nine volunteers," he said. "But I warn you, it won't be too flash out there."

"Oh, who cares about that. Where will we be staying?"

"Probably in shearers' quarters on a rural property." Alex replied. "We'll have to be totally self-sufficient – take our own food and cook for ourselves. The most I can offer is transport out there and a bed to sleep in, and long days digging in the dirt. But, hopefully, it will be an opportunity to find some seriously old bones, dinosaur bones, that haven't seen the light of day for almost a hundred million years. Still interested?" he asked.

"Absolutely." Denise beamed at him, her eyes alight with excitement.

Alex returned her grin. "I knew I could count on you."

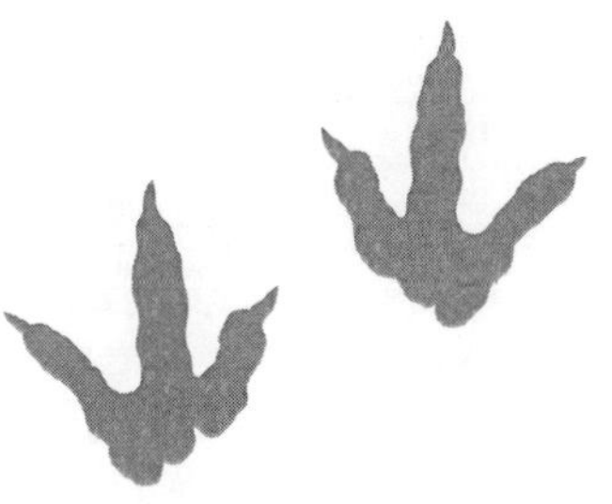

CHAPTER 5

That night Denise had dinner with her favourite nephew, Daniel. She and Dan ate together on Wednesday nights when his mother was teaching night classes. Denise had enjoyed a close relationship with him since he was a baby, and had read dinosaur books to him when he was a toddler. Dan was fascinated with the long complicated names, and learned to pronounce them all. He liked to sound out the words and enjoyed the way they rolled off his tongue. 'Saur–o–pod. Ther–o–pod.' As he got older they had researched dinosaurs, googling dinosaur finds in America, and lately in China. But, to their disappointment, there had been very few fossils found in Australia.

Denise shared her exciting news with Dan. Not only had a large dinosaur bone been found in Australia, right here in Queensland, but she had been offered a chance to go on a dig.

"That's awesome! It would be so cool to find a dinosaur nobody has ever seen before! That would be legendary! I wish I could go too!" he enthused.

Dan had been volunteering at the Queensland Museum with Denise on weekends. His career advisor was talking about subject choices and careers, and Dan was seriously considering palaeontology as a career. He was hoping to get some work experience at the Queensland Museum in the future.

"I guess it will be an adults only trip," he said. "And probably not in the school holidays."

Denise noted the disappointment in his voice. He might be right, but she resolved to ask Alex some questions next time she saw him, and to see what she could do. They changed the subject and talked about other things.

■■■

The next time Denise saw Alex she asked how plans for the dig were going.

"Have you got enough volunteers?" she asked.

"Still looking for a couple more," he said. "Timing isn't good – it'll be during the school holidays and a lot of people can't make it then as they have children to look after."

"Would you consider taking a work experience student? Someone who is already volunteering at the museum?" She paused, trying to gauge his reaction.

"You mean Daniel, your nephew?" he asked.

"Yes. He's very keen and he's considering palaeontology as a career."

Alex paused, studying Denise's face. "I doubt the museum would take responsibility for a school student away from the museum buildings."

"I'd be responsible for him – and I'd pay for whatever extras we'd need if he could go."

Alex thought for a moment. "I can ask. I know he's a good worker, and very responsible for his age. And if you're prepared to sign a waiver and take responsibility for him they may consider it."

"I'd be grateful if you would ask. He's very keen."

■■■

A week later she got the word from Alex that, if Denise was prepared to sign the relevant paperwork, Daniel could join the dig. She knew his mother would be okay with that, and Daniel would be ecstatic.

And he was! When Denise broke the news to him he could hardly believe it was true. Not only was he considered responsible enough to join the dig team, but his favourite aunt thought enough of him to want to sponsor him and take him along. He was going on a dig to try and find what could be Australia's largest dinosaur.

But what if they came back empty handed...?

CHAPTER 6

David raced into the kitchen to pick up the ringing phone. He was expecting the stock truck driver to call to let him know when the trucks would arrive at Belmont.

"Hi David, this is Alex," the voice said. "I've got it sorted – the dig is on! We'll be there in August."

It was a month since Alex had left Belmont, determined to see if he could organise a dig to try and find more dinosaur bones.

"I have a dig crew of eight, and me of course," he continued. "We'll all be coming from Brisbane, so is it still okay to use the shearers' quarters?"

"Absolutely," responded David. "Just let me know the dates in August and I'll get Judy to get it sorted. Plenty of room, and I'll organise some equipment as well." So it was actually going to happen!

But life on the station had to continue as usual. There were cattle and sheep to look after and fences to mend. However, David often found his thoughts going back to the conversation with Alex that night around the dinner table. He tried to imagine herds of dinosaurs, some fifteen or twenty metres long, grazing where his cattle were now foraging. Alex said they were herbivores, so there must have been an enormous amount of vegetation around for them to survive. Quite different to now.

And what did they look like? Were there different types of dinosaurs? There must have been. Surely sauropods weren't the only dinosaurs in Australia. It would be like believing his sheep were the only animals out here – no cattle, or kangaroos, or dogs. No, there must have been other types.

Every time David rode out on his motorbike now he looked at the rocks in the paddocks differently. Were they really rocks, or were they dinosaur bones in hiding? It took enormous willpower for him not to stop at every interesting looking rock and roll it over to see if he could detect a fossil. The word was spreading around the area and some of his neighbours had already said they thought they had found bones on their properties.

But he had a sheep and cattle property to run, and now he had a group or people arriving in a month or so to do a dig. He had machinery and tools to organise. This was a big country and he didn't think they were going to find anything if they just went out there with shovels. He would get the grader and the bobcat ready. If there were more bones lying out there they would hopefully be as big as the bone he had already found.

■■■

August came, and late one afternoon the dig team arrived. David and Judy settled them into the shearers' quarters. They were a mixed lot – men and women and one teenager. Apart from Alex, none of them had been this far west before. They stood around outside the shearers' quarters looking out on the flat paddocks that stretched to the horizon. They were obviously a bit overwhelmed with the open space and the distances in the outback.

David sat with Alex that evening, away from the group, discussing how they would go about the dig.

"We'll need to establish a grid pattern around the area where that bone was found, and dig a series of holes to see if we can locate anything else," said Alex. "When we find something we can carefully excavate around it with trowels."

David looked sceptical. He had his doubts. "That might not work," he said. "We could dig hundreds of holes and find nothing. This country is so big, and didn't you say we only have a few days?"

"Yeah, we have to leave here in ten days."

"What if we dig a hole and it's a metre too far to the left of a bone or a metre too far to the right – we could miss it. There could be a bone in the middle and we'd never know. It's a bit like looking for a needle in a haystack," David argued.

It was Alex's turn to look sceptical.

"This is a big country Alex. We need to quickly cover a large area, and then if we find something we can work more slowly and more carefully," reasoned David. "I can use the grader to scrape off the soil a few inches at a time until we find something interesting."

Finally Alex relented. David's idea certainly was not normal practice at a fossil dig where they would usually work carefully using small tools.

"Okay – I hear you, so let's compromise. We'll dig a few exploratory holes by hand first to see if we can find anything. If we don't find anything in the first five or six holes you can bring in the grader," he agreed.

"Sounds like a plan. I'll get the grader out there tomorrow." But David kept his worries to himself. This was a seriously big country, and what if they didn't find anything...

CHAPTER 7

It was hot and dusty and dirty. Denise and Dan had expected that, but the flies that hung around their faces all the time were extremely annoying. Some people had bought fly nets, a cover made of fine mesh that fitted over their hats. Dan thought they looked weird, but they did stop the flies crawling around your eyes and up your nose.

But the team was there to do some serious work in the next ten days before they had to return to Brisbane. Some people had to go back to work, and Dan had to go back to school. And they all definitely, absolutely, wanted to find some dinosaur bones.

They were a group of eight – nine if you counted Alex. They were bunked in at the shearers' quarters, and Denise and Dan were sharing a room off the main kitchen with a set of almost comfortable bunk beds. Not that it mattered, as they were both so tired at the end of the day, they fell asleep as soon as their heads hit the pillow. The showers were hot and strong, the food tasty and there was plenty of it. Dan approved, even if it did mean sharing a bedroom with his aunt.

What Dan wasn't prepared for was the sheer size of the country. The sky seemed to go on forever and the grassland paddocks were huge. The paddock where they were to dig must have been a hundred hectares or more. How they knew exactly where to dig amazed him.

He was even more amazed at the size of the machinery. In his mind he had imagined they would be using little pick-like gardening tools and maybe some screwdrivers. But David, the farmer, had a grader. A great big road-making grader!

The first day they pegged out an area, dug a few holes and found nothing. The next day David drove the grader over the ground, scraping off a few centimetres of soil and heaping it up to one side. Dan's job, along with the others, was to walk at the edges of the grader blade watching for anything the blade might disturb. If they saw anything they were to shout out and David would stop the grader so they could investigate.

But nothing surfaced, and it was hot and dusty and dry. Nothing but a few rocks and sticks, and tomorrow would be day three.

■■■

The next day they hit pay dirt! Just after morning tea the shout went up. Dan had been taking his turn walking beside the left edge of the grader blade watching the soil curl away when something hard flicked out of the ground.

"Stop," yelled Dan. "Over there – there's something over there!"

David stopped the grader immediately and Alex raced over to investigate. With his expert eye he identified patterns that indicated this rock was indeed a fossilised bone.

"Jackpot. Well spotted Dan!" Alex clapped him on the back. "I think we're on to something good!"

David carefully backed the grader away and brought in the bobcat. Centimetre by centimetre he excavated a hole, starting a few metres away from the spot where the bone had emerged. He stopped every time the shout went up, indicating there was something unusual in the soil.

By lunchtime they had a hole Alex was happy with. There were quite a few traces of fossilised bone fragments that could be an indication there were some serious bones to be found. This area would be worth excavating further.

Over the lunch break the men erected a tent fly over the site so they could work in the shade. Alex put pegs around the site and established a grid so any bones found could be mapped on a plan of the dig site. Each digger was allocated an area on the grid to excavate slowly and carefully. Dan and Denise were to work together in grid sector 4J. They were instructed to call Alex the moment they found something.

Dan was excited and amazed. Here, in Queensland, he was finding bones from dinosaurs. Bones that had been buried for 100 million years...

CHAPTER 8

David was elated. He excitedly told Judy about the find.

"That first rock – when it came out of the ground – I knew, I just knew it was a dinosaur bone! I just knew there were more bones down there."

Judy had not been at the dig site that morning as there were jobs to be done on the farm. But she knew David had been worried they would not find anything and the team of diggers would go home disappointed.

"But it's so slow," he continued. "Alex is so careful when they find something. Everyone has to work so carefully, and every piece found has to be marked on his plan of the dig site. But he's in charge and he's a palaeontologist, so he knows all about excavating sites."

Both he and Judy had wondered how many bones would be found in the few days of the dig. Progress was frustratingly slow, but that was the way it had to be done. David wondered if they would find some big bones, bones that would fit together to make up a skeleton or even parts of a skeleton. And he wondered if they would all be from one dinosaur, or would there be bones from more than one dinosaur buried here?

David spent all day out at the dig, watching and helping where he could. There was no need for big machinery now. They were concentrating on this one area where every hour they found more bone fragments. Alex had to be called to each find, and he carefully measured and then plotted the position of each item on his dig plan. The bigger pieces were carefully wrapped in tin foil, newspaper and finally a layer of plaster of Paris so they could be safely transported to a safe dry location where they could be 'prepped' – the painstaking task of chipping or grinding rock away from the fossil.

"So how long does it take to prep a bone?" David asked Alex.

"Months, mate, even years," replied Alex. "It's a very slow process and we use fine drills – the sort of drills dentists use. At the Queensland Museum we only have a couple of people who can do it, and we want to build up a team of volunteers to help. We have years of work waiting, so we only work on significant bones at the moment."

"Just as well they're already 100 million years old and fossilised, and they won't deteriorate further," said David. "They're not going to go off."

"Well, actually they do," replied Alex. "While they're buried in the dirt they're well supported and kept cool. When we dig then up they're exposed to the air for the first time in millions of years. The risk is they can get fragile and brittle, so we encase the bigger bones in a plaster cast to protect them. Bit like we do for someone with a broken bone."

“Except these bones aren’t going to heal,” laughed David. But he did wonder, if they did find lots of bones, how many would actually be investigated...

CHAPTER 9

It had been the most awesome week of Dan's life. Each day they found more bones. Each day there were more exciting discoveries. But day six proved to be outstanding.

The fossilised bones they were finding were big, the remains of a large dinosaur. Alex said he was fairly sure it was a sauropod or maybe several sauropods. It was too early to tell as the fragments needed to be prepped before they could be fitted together. It was not until prepping was completed that they could be definitely identified. Hopefully some of the bones would fit together. It was like an enormous jigsaw puzzle, but nobody knew how many pieces were there, or how many pieces were missing.

Every night at the shearing shed they talked over dinner. Was it one animal or several? It was obviously from a big dinosaur. If Alex's estimation proved to be right, it was around fifteen metres long. How old was it? How did it die?

■■■

Day six changed everything.

Dan was carefully excavating around a bone when an unusual shape began to emerge. It was smaller and more delicate than the other fragments around it. It had a peculiar curve making it quite different to most of the other straight and chunky bones he had found. Dan showed Denise who called Alex over.

"Wow!" exclaimed Alex excitedly. He immediately called a halt. Carefully, ever so carefully, he prised the bone away from the soil and carried it over to the makeshift examination table. The group gathered around as he examined the fossil with great care. But it was not a bone. The shape of the curve was a perfect arc, and on one small area the rock had fallen away, exposing a grey-brown smooth surface with a shine to it. There was no doubt about it – it was not a bone, it was a claw! And sauropods did not have claws! So this was a fossilised claw from a meat eating dinosaur. A theropod.

There were two dinosaurs in this hole. One a herbivore, one a carnivore.

So what had happened here?

Dan could only imagine. He dreamed at night of dinosaurs roaming the plains. So there definitely was a range of different dinosaurs in Australia 100 million years ago. But what happened here, at Winton, all those eons ago?

He knew sauropods were huge plant eating dinosaurs. He knew theropods were meat eaters, and he also knew they were a lot smaller than sauropods. Much smaller – not much bigger than a large man. It is very hard to imagine a theropod trying to kill a sauropod for food. Surely it would not take on an animal so much bigger than itself? Surely it would look for something smaller?

So what happened here? How did they end up in the same grave?

Dan drifted off to sleep wondering.

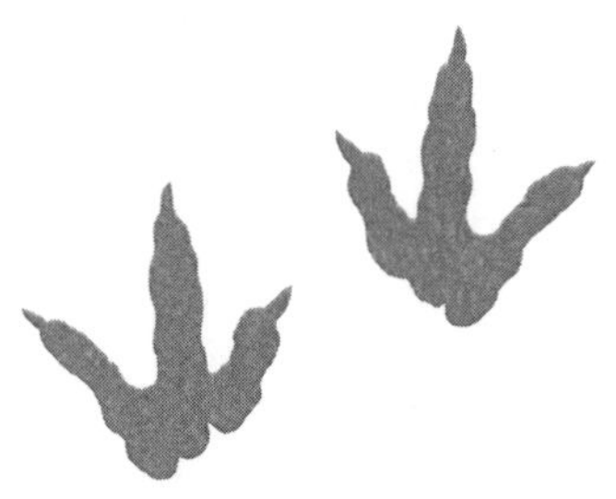

CHAPTER 10

It was the last day in January, not that Matilda would have known. With a brain seriously small in relation to their size, sauropods were not designed to think a great deal – not beyond their immediate environment anyway. Thinking was related to food and water and shelter. As one of the biggest animals, they did not have to worry about safety. Very few animals would mess with them. So it was mostly about food, water and survival.

But Matilda did know the rains had not come as they usually did. The waterholes were receding and the cycads were dropping their leaves. Her diet was not as soft as it used to be, and did not contain as much moisture, and lush green vegetation was harder to find. When you are over fifteen metres long and weigh almost twenty tonnes, and you are a vegetarian, this is a pretty important issue.

Matilda had experienced drought before. She had moved to other places where there were not so many animals competing for the same food. But she was older now, and pregnant. She had been pregnant before, so knew she would have to take it easy until she laid her egg. She knew she needed extra food and extra water. Her huge legs ached and she felt bone weary. She did not want to walk for days, so she would stay here.

The other sauropods had moved on to find more abundant food supplies. That was the way it always happened – the stronger animals, especially the males, would move on to find easier food. The old, the sick and the pregnant sauropods would hang behind and make do with what was still edible. They either survived on a minimal diet until the rains came, or they died. Those who were pregnant laid their eggs and would then hope to re-join the others. That was just the way it was.

The last three waterholes Matilda had visited were dry. They were in areas where small pools and lakes normally filled from streams that ran down the gullies. But the streams hadn't flowed for months. The rains, when they came last rainy season, had not lasted long enough or been heavy enough to get the rivers flowing beyond a trickle. Gradually the creeks had dried up completely.

There was some moisture in the leaves she was eating. Matilda tended to stay out of the direct sun under the shade of the conifers during the day and forage for food in the early morning and late afternoon.

The combination of reduced food and water and the fact that she was pregnant was making Matilda feel tired. Once she had laid her egg she would be able to walk faster and maybe catch up with the other sauropods. In the meantime she knew she had to find a supply of water. There was one waterhole she remembered not far from her present location that she had visited once before. It was in a depression between two rock faces. The river, when it did flow, had worn quite a deep hole in the bottom of the gully. It was the lowest point in the valley and water tended to collect there. The only problem was the gully was quite narrow and normally the sauropods would not go there to drink. The steep banks were difficult for large animals to get up and down. They preferred wider areas of water where they could navigate their huge bodies without any risk of getting stuck. But those areas tended to be shallower, and were now mostly dried up.

Matilda decided she would go to the gully and check it out...

CHAPTER 11

Matilda was not alone in her search for water.

There were many types of dinosaurs in the area and one, a small to medium-sized carnivore, was also on the hunt for a drink. Banjo was a semi-upright, theropod dinosaur. Standing about a metre and a half tall, he ran on his strong hind legs and used his front limbs to attack. Later, much later, he would be given the fancy name of Australavenator, but right now he was just Banjo and he was thirsty.

Banjo normally dined on much smaller dinosaurs. His powerful back legs allowed him to run very fast, and the massive talons on his front legs could strike down and maim with great speed and accuracy. His sharp ripping teeth could then tear his prey into bite sized pieces. A perfectly designed killing machine.

Banjo had experienced a rough summer. He would normally hunt alone, stalking and then hunting down smaller dinosaurs. His favourite prey were small ornithopods (bird-like dinosaurs) that travelled in packs. He could chase a group of them, causing panic, and then pick off the slow and weak at the back of the pack. But as the waterholes had begun to dry up there were fewer around, and there was also more competition from other theropods in the area. As carnivores they were all looking for the same food.

He normally would not hunt with other theropods, but on occasions when he did, it provided the opportunity to chase and then divide a pack of ornithopods. They would scatter in all directions and in the chaos and confusion it was possible to kill and eat well. He had joined a group of theropods hunting in a lake area that had been reduced to a sea of mud. The ground was soft and sticky, and it was difficult to run fast. But then the ornithopods couldn't run as fast either.

They had herded a group of ornithopods into a gully so they could go in for the kill. Banjo had slipped in the mud and twisted his leg. The leg was badly bruised, the ligaments were torn, and he was in pain. But fortunately it was not broken – that would have been a death sentence for Banjo. He could still walk but no longer run fast to capture his prey. The other theropods left him and continued their hunt, and he was reduced to picking over the leftovers of animals others had killed. And they didn't leave much; they too were hungry. He had to resort to stalking old and dying animals until they were too weak to run away. That was not only time consuming, it often meant following a weak animal for days hoping to feed on the carcass before any other predators got there and threatened him. Not the way he liked to live, but food is food, and when you are hungry you take what you can get.

But right now he needed to find a waterhole and, if he was lucky, there might be an animal he could hunt down to eat...

CHAPTER 12

The gully was much as Matilda remembered it. Narrow, so sheltered from the sun most of the day by the overhanging cliffs. At one point it was so narrow her enormous belly almost touched both sides. At the waterhole the gully opened up to what was almost an oasis. In a good rainy season the waterhole would have taken up the entire width of the gully, but now it was only half the size. But there was some water in it. And there were healthy leafy plants growing around the edge that would provide a great source of food for her for quite a while. Good find.

Banjo had come up from the lower side of the gully. Water, lovely water. He had smelled it from quite a long way away. He was surprised to see Matilda drinking there. As far as he knew the sauropods had all left the area a while ago. Lack of vegetation meant this was not a good place for a sauropod to be.

Banjo surveyed the area around the waterhole. Here there were still a lot of green plants. Matilda was on the far edge where the bank was not as steep. She was no threat to him, nor he to her. As a vegetarian she was not interested in him as a meal, and she was far too big for him to attack her. Even a large group of theropods would not tackle a sauropod. The enormous size and weight of a sauropod would deter even the hungriest hunter. There was always more suitable prey around. Other animals would come to the waterhole that would provide an easier meal.

So Banjo and Matilda drank from opposite sides of the waterhole. It was cool. They would stay for a while.

■■■

Matilda had taken advantage of the vegetation around the edge of the gully. A full belly and a good drink had made her feel a lot happier. She was working on a plan. The far side of the waterhole opened out to a wider gully. Water was seeping down the gully a fair distance, and there appeared to be vegetation growing further downstream. An underground spring was keeping the area moist, allowing the plants to thrive. This was looking like a good place to stay until she was ready to lay her egg, and then she could leave and catch up with the other sauropods. If she crossed the waterhole and grazed her way down the gully, staying within reach of water, she could probably survive for a couple of weeks or even a month, maybe even longer if she was careful. And if the rains came maybe the other sauropods would return and she wouldn't have to leave.

Banjo was not feeling so optimistic. He was getting hungry, desperately hungry. He had hoped smaller animals would come to the waterhole and he would be able to prey on them. But none had come to his side of the waterhole, or had come and gone so quickly he had not had a chance to go in for the kill. His leg was still painful and he could not move fast. He was getting very hungry. Extremely hungry...

CHAPTER 13

Matilda had to make a move. The water in the waterhole had receded significantly in the days since she had arrived, and she had stripped almost all of the greenery from the plants on her side of the waterhole. She could see more vegetation on the other side and further down the gully, and she was hungry.

She was wary of stepping into the waterhole. Normally sauropods were very careful around water. It was better to stand well clear of the edge and lower their long necks down into the water to drink, keeping their bodies well clear and on stable ground. She had once seen one of her herd get stuck in a muddy waterhole, and die a pretty horrible death. She had been warned and she was wary, but right now she didn't have any other options. There was no other way to get to the vegetation on the other side of the waterhole.

Tentatively Matilda tested the mud at the edge of the waterhole. Her huge legs sank into the mud, but the bottom felt fairly solid. The waterhole was probably only fifteen metres across – about the length of her body. Five, six, seven, maybe ten steps and she would be across.

Her twenty tonnes of weight compressed the mud under her feet as she stepped forward. It seemed to get softer as she moved further in. Maybe it was just the rotted vegetation on the bottom of the waterhole. One more step, and then another step, and then another and she would be clear.

Matilda felt herself slipping. As she lost her balance her body slipped sideways into the water and her bulk caused her to roll onto her side. Her massive weight pushed her shoulder and hip deep into the mud. Fortunately she could keep her head above the water – her long neck helped. Valiantly Matilda tried to get her legs back underneath her, but the oozy sticky mud made that impossible.

The more Matilda struggled the worse the situation became. The mud seemed to suck at her and trap her. Her body was not designed for this – all her muscles were built to move her around when upright. On her side she did not have the strength to push, and her joints did not work that way. She sensed she was in trouble, big trouble.

Banjo watched from the shade on the opposite bank of the waterhole. This was something unusual. He didn't expect this to happen. Maybe it was the opportunity he had been waiting for...

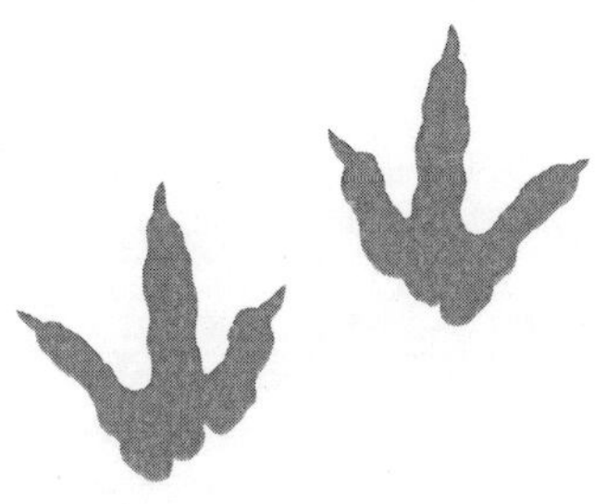

CHAPTER 14

Matilda was getting weaker. Three days of struggling had sapped her energy. Her heart was pounding in her chest. In the last day she had been unable to move at all, apart from her neck.

Banjo was still watching. He watched Matilda become weaker, her movements more feeble. He knew he was no match for a sauropod, but maybe if she got weak enough, or if she died, there would be an answer to his hunger problem.

So he watched. And he waited. And he was still hungry, extremely hungry.

Finally, it looked like the time was right. Matilda had not moved all afternoon. Dusk was falling, and all was quiet. Banjo made his way carefully around the edge of the waterhole to the area where Matilda had eaten away the vegetation. He knew instinctively the best way to kill was to go for the throat. This is what he did with the ornithopods he killed. Stay away from the legs – they usually had claws. Go for the throat. That makes for an easy kill. And less danger for him.

Matilda saw movement out of the corner of her eye. She was weak but she was still aware of her surroundings. She watched as Banjo crept along the edge of the waterhole towards her head, leaving distinctive three toed footprints in the mud. She watched as he stood and judged how far he would have to leap to get to her. She watched as he tensed his legs, getting ready to launch himself at her. She was ready and waiting...

The strike was quick. Banjo had calculated the distance and had balanced his body ready to go in for the kill. But he had not taken into account the strength and the length of Matilda's neck.

She saw him leap. She saw he was favouring his injured leg, and so could not leap straight. He swayed to the left, leaving the side of his body exposed to her. Instead of attacking front on he had to twist his head to latch onto her throat.

With all the strength Matilda could muster she flung her head up striking Banjo on his side, her neck smashing across his sore leg. He spun in the air. Unable to control himself he went into free-fall across her massive body, landing in the mud beside her. His injured leg was beneath him and he couldn't move. Pain, so much pain – his leg was broken.

Exhausted, Matilda laid her head back into the mud. She did not have the strength to lift it clear and the mud filled her nostrils and blocked her airway. Matilda was gone.

Banjo, stunned by the blow, stared at the side of the pool – the mud, the vegetation. The light failed as dusk set in. He was trapped. He had nowhere to go. Banjo had tried his best and lost.

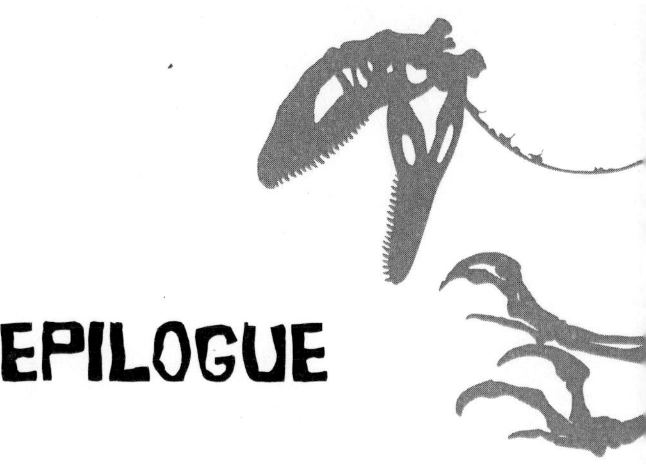

EPILOGUE

News of the confirmed dinosaur find in outback Queensland spread rapidly. Within months more dinosaur fossils were found on properties in the area. The black soil is a major factor in this, as when black soil expands during a wet season it has the effect of 'squeezing' any bones to the surface. Landholders, aware of the initial find at Belmont, now take more interest in exposed 'rocks' on their properties. That is why the year after a big rain is now called a 'dinosaur hunters' season'. The remains of many more dinosaurs have been found including Elliot, Wade, Matt, Dixie, Mary, Bob, Chooky, Pete, Jenna, Mogi, Ian, Mick and Ollie.

■■■

The theropod and sauropod found together in the dig site in this book were given the nick names Banjo and Matilda after the Australian poet Banjo Patterson and characters from his works. Banjo Patterson wrote his famous ballad 'Waltzing Matilda' while in the Winton area.

■■■

The digs that revealed the bones of Matilda and Banjo continued from 2006 until 2010. Teams of diggers came to work and excavated more bones. Bones from the digs are still being prepped, but enough material has already been completed and identified to allow Scott Hucknull, Senior Curator at the Queensland Museum, to formally identify both Matilda and Banjo as new species of dinosaurs unique to Australia.

MATILDA

Diamantinasaurus matildae (Dye-ah-man-teen-ah-sor-us mah-til-day)

Length: 15–16 metres

Height: 2.5 metres at the hip

Weight: 15–20 tonnes

Bones illustrated are those formally identified as of 2009. (More have been formally identified since then.)

BANJO

Australovenator wintonensis (Oss-tra-low-ven-ah-tor win-ton-en-sis)

Length: 5 metres

Height: 1.5 metres at the hip

Weight: 500 kg

Bones illustrated are those formally identified as of 2009. (More have been formally identified since then.)

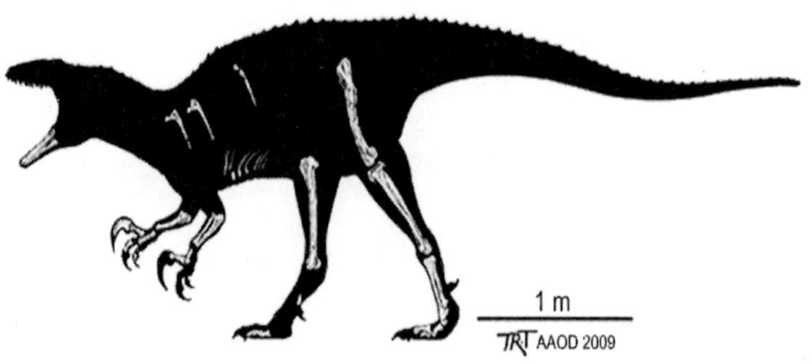

THE DIG SITE

Analysis of the dig site and the layout of the bones suggests that both animals died in the billabong at the same time. This picture shows the position of the bones of Matilda and Banjo as they were found at the dig site.

AUSTRALIAN AGE OF DINOSAURS

David and Judy Elliot organised shed space at Belmont Station where fossils in plaster jackets could be stored. They also encouraged volunteer preppers to travel to Belmont, stay in the shearers' quarters, and work on the bones. As the number of fossil finds increased, and the numbers of preppers increased, it became obvious larger storage facilities and more prep areas were needed.

David and Judy went on to form the Australian Age of Dinosaurs (AAOD), a not-for-profit organisation. A local farmer donated land near Winton. A building program is underway on this land. Stage One (prep and support area) and Stage Two (reception and display area) have been completed. Stage Three (outdoor galleries and Museum of Natural History) is under construction.

The bones of Matilda and Banjo can be seen at the AAOD site where teams of preppers are still finishing the last of the bones taken from the Banjo and Matilda digs. There are currently more than ten years of bones waiting to be prepped, and more are dug up every year at a number of on-going digs in the area.

Come and have a look. Check out the bones and watch preppers in action. It is even possible to become a prepper yourself. There are hundreds of bones waiting!